Breathe, Heal, Grow

Collection of Poems

S. N. Butler

BookLeaf Publishing

India | USA | UK

Dedication

For every reader who finds a piece of themselves within these poems. May you find your light within the darkness.

Preface

My life has had so many ups and downs. Poetry and writing has always been a way I've delt with situations and feelings. The poems I have written in this book were inspired by my own healing journey. My past, although at times rough, is what has made me who I am today. Although challenging, I am proud of who I am and where I brought myself and my daughter. Life will continue to have its challenges, and we all face different versions of them. My hope for this book is to be able to help someone see they are not alone in their journey. No matter what your challenge is, or what your trauma might be, you can face it. That view at the end is worth it.

Acknowledgements

To my family, who love me through my pains.

To my friends, who push me every day to live my dreams.

And most importantly, to my daughter, who is my inspiration for everything I do in life.

Thank you all for your continuous support and love throughout my struggles and dreams. Without you, none of this would be possible.

1. New Life

There were days where the darkness you brought
drowned out my light,
Days that I spent filled with your night.
That anger that brought fear and controlled my every
move,
No matter what in my life I tried to do.
You were there for years pretending to be
What I truly thought was the only version to see.
Yet there was more hiding behind that door,
Which you covered from me until it was ready to pour.
Like flood gates it would come,
In more phases than one.
An unstoppable force
Needing to run its course.
Yet I could not run from the pain
That came in waves ready to stain,
Or the crippling fear
That would bring me to tears.
This darkness loomed,
All because I was groomed,
And trained to believe
There was nothing else for me.
Which I did, every word,
No matter what was poured.

From lies to hate,
And whatever came late.
Yet the scariest part was
When the darkness turned to fuzz,
And the moment that existed,
Now was seemingly twisted.
For the darkness that was there
Was no longer shared,
And instead a fabricated thought
Was all that you brought.
Yet the truth still lingered
No matter where you pointed your finger
Until you made it hard to see
Past all the problems being me.
So I tried to be better, quiet, and less
Trying to fix something that wasn't my mess
Yet I believed when you said I was the issue.
Even in moments I tried to pursue,
And changed myself to make it better
Sticking who I was in the shredder.
Until I couldn't recognize
The girl in the mirror staring in my eyes
I became a stranger to me
And hid the parts I loved to be
Yet something awoke in my soul
The moment I realized the lies you told
And just how far you were willing to go

To make sure I would not continue to grow
For my success you saw as your failure
And showed it with your behavior
I was tired of being your net
That caught all your darkness and threats
With none of my concerns heard
As you ignored every word
So I found my way out
From that lifeless drought
Not just to be free
But so I could also find me
As I have spent years hiding who I am
And I no longer want to give a damn
Because the me that I miss is the one that you hated
And yes she may be a little bit faded
But she is clawing, trying to find her way out
And when she does, there is no doubt
The girl you forced me to become
Will be the one I force to succumb.

2. Cry Myself to Sleep

As I cry myself to sleep
My heart sinkers deeper as it weeps
For happy times I do not miss
But events that never did exist
And as you lay awake and loud
You reminded me why I am proud
Because I left when it was easier to stay
And now I'm no longer just your prey.
So yes I cried myself to sleep
But not for the words you spoke to me
I cried as a reminder of all those years
You manipulated lies to control my fears
Yet now my fears no longer involve you
And unlike you, I already grew.

3. Future Reality

My vision is filled with endless banter
On past lives that no longer seem to matter
And doors that have closed sooner than expected
Yet the one left open is where I am directed
Where life seemed so blissfully sweet
And time, standing still, felt complete
No worries crossed the mind
As no worries were yet assigned
And dreams were a blissful thought
The more ideas that they brought
Yet life has a funny way
Of making those dreams portray
A different reality than in my mind
One that feels more confined
And the space between reality and imagination
Seems to have lacked in communication
For I did not define this life of mine
More so it seems to be assigned
As pieces start fitting one by one
Like my spinning wheel has already spun
And I drift along this written course
Like a river with its force
And wait to see the new beginning
Hoping this time I might be winning

But I do not have control of the waves
Or the way this river behaves
Although I could attempt to fight
And swim away just in spite
It would only make the moment tougher
And just cause me to suffer
Yet I know I could also ride the river
And wait to see what she may deliver
Having faith in the plan at hand
Even if I do not understand
For faith is trusting through blindness
Even with no true guidance
And understanding that your life's purpose
Is far more than you can surface
So I trust in fate to reveal its plan
As it's been trying since this began
And I understand that my exact dreams may not come
But the dream that does was always the better one

4. Mr. Moon

Dear Mr. Moon
Like you, I go through phases too.
One moment I shine as bright as the stars,
And other times, it's easier to see Jupiter or Mars.
Yet, unlike you, I can not completely hide my face
Even if there are days I wish it could be misplaced.
No, instead I'm pushed to portray the sun
Whose bright light is meant to guide everyone.
And although I know I should feel blessed,
Even the big bright sun gets its rest.
Yet, Mr. Moon, my soul does get wary
But I won't ever show just how much it carries.
And when days turn to nights and your face finally glows,
Remember I'm just like you Mr.Moon, even if no one knows.

5. Life's Trail

Life has thrown me all around
Head up straight, knees on the ground.
Yet here I am trying to find,
The voice that calls me back inside.
And yet my soul still chooses to wander,
Which leaves my mind continuing to ponder,
Ways to live soullessly free,
Or ways this world may defeat me.
In truth I know nether are choices,
But neither is listening to all of the voices.
For the sounds always mingled all together,
And I never know which one was better.
So I go to hear the trees,
The silence filled with just the breeze.
And as I'm guided through its maze,
My soul no longer wants to stray.
I begin to feel myself become whole,
Although I may still lack control,
But I continue deeper just to see,
If this may begin to heal me.
And though my legs grew tired on the trail,
My heart in ways began to inhale.
So with eyes closed I began to listen,
To the sounds my heart and soul was missin'.

And the peace that filled around me,
Began to place me down so soundly.
Back into the world I did know,
Reminding me I will continue to grow.
Though the growth can come in pains,
The ending chapter still remains.
And much like the pains on a trail,
If you stopped to turn around and bail,
You may never see what's waiting for you,
Because until the end, there is no view.

6. Lost Light

She fell from grace as soon as she stood,
A disgrace she felt as hard as she could.
Yet when she sat all she felt was numb,
So this feeling was still more welcome than none.
Her eyes filled deeper with pain and longing,
Wanting to feel that sense of belonging.
And as she continued to stand hands by her side,
She felt the pull to take that first stride.
Through her darkness she continued on,
Hoping she soon would find the dawn,
Yet darkness can be thick and blinding,
And she soon feared of never finding,
That light she so desperately fought to see,
The light she needed to finally be free.
So she continued through the black,
While her faith and hope began to lack.
And as each moment began to fade,
She began to wish that she hadn't strayed.
So far from the path she was originally on,
Yet that path now was so far gone.
With legs no longer willing to keep moving,
She ponder sitting once more begging the darkness to
stop consuming.
But she knew sitting would surely take her back,

To a life she knew where her heart would lack.
Where the numbness would welcome her like a distant
cousin,
In attempts to mask the pain and tenderness that would
come all of a sudden.
Yet pain is what drew her to stand,
And the desire to live was brought back to her hands.
She felt the need become a strong force,
As a hunger in her soul began to course.
And she looked back at the darkness still around,
Beginning to scream because she wasn't found,
Yet the more she screamed and yelled and cursed,
The more she felt the darkness disburse.
So she allowed every feeling she pushed down,
To come back up and no longer be bound,
And through the anger, tears, yells and screams,
A small light began to gleam.
She let every feeling push through,
And so that light only grew.
A fire so bright it could burn the sun,
She soon witnessed the darkness begin to run.
And as she looked at her new path, clear and strong,
She realized the light she's been looking for was in her
all along.

7. My Sun

I find my sun behind the shade
Of where I once was laid
Long ago on the floor
Until I left and closed that door
Yet here I stand with just a crack
No desire to go back
Yet the darkness still finds a way
To keep me in its grasp and stay
As clouds begin to cover my sun
Making me believe this is all done
But my desire still ignites the fire
Even if peace was once the liar
As true peace does not have conditions
Yet instead should light ambitions
So I wait for the sun to shine
As it is part of their design
For clouds to swarm and create darkness
Yet even the clouds can't truly harness
The light the sun shines from behind
And the cracks in the clouds the light will find
Out it pours its golden rays
Reminding the darkness that it stays
Even if it tries to hover
Not all light can be covered

For mine knows the clouds must move
Even if the timing can be hard to prove

13

8. The Change

My days have been spent with ways to ignite my soul,

My nights have been used for pondering plans to make me whole.

And yet in every moment I'm reminded how empty the world feels

Even though I know what it is truly trying to reveal.

And yet I fight, run, plead, and break,

Just praying for my soul to take

One last look at where we are

One last look, please, we've come so far.

Yet it whispers as it begins to look away

"Who are you to think we deserve to stay?"

So with legs too weak to run anymore,

I drop my knees down to the forests floor.

My eyes so heavy as their own rivers flow

I begin to feel every door open that was closed long ago

And as every crack began to shatter and break,

I felt the Earth below me begin to quake.

Even my fear of the unknown could not stop this force

And once again i heard my soul tell me "let it run its course"

So I sat, still, in the chaotic silence

Waiting for any additional guidance

Yet, again, my soul went quiet

But this time I decided not to be defiant.
And I sat, for days that felt like years
Letting the ground soak in all my tears.
With my eyes closed so tight, l faded away
Until one day, I felt my soul begin to sway.
"Look now" it sang loud and slow
"Look and see just how much has grown"
But my eyes wouldn't open for fear of what it might see
Fear that there would be nothing left of me.
Yet the voice rang once more deep in my chest,
No longer willing to remain suppressed.
And as my eyes opened I could see
What all that chaos was around me.
What was once a forest filled with dirt and dying trees,
Became a meadow of rivers, wildflowers, and bees.
And as I sat admiring the view and the stars,
I began to find the beauty in all these scars.
It was in this moment I was overcome with relief,
Because for the first time in forever, I felt my soul
breathe.

9. My Ocean, Your Sand

Here is where I choose to be
Right where the land meets the sea
Waves crashing against the sand
Then pulls back, away from the land
Gentle strokes of natures pure passion
And yet even sometimes they are rationed
For the moon pulls back a little here and there
Before coming closer and choosing to share
And those waves may slow or grow more wild
No desire to become mild
Watching just how each one teases
Although even that still pleases
As winds provoke the waves to crash
And the moon reminds it just how to act
The sand obeys and does what it's told
Though it still plays and becomes somewhat bold
As portions mix back in with the water
Hoping it will last just a few moments longer
And deep within that tide they remain
Until the wave no longer wishes to maintain
With the ocean being calmer than the land
It can't help but to expand
So the sand settles where it's left
Happy in its little quest

Engulfed by the oceans pure beauty
Down where its roomy
And views of life all around
A new world filed with different sounds
And as the sea continued to meet the shore
The sand pours in even more
Glistening the tide with its salty surface
Renditioning its true life's purpose
For the ocean and the sand are one in the same
And together, each other, they will always claim

10. Behind the Mask

With my face covered in little shards
Of past traumas and mending scars
Enough to cover my full existence
And hide myself in an instant
So with every piece of me that falls
I use to help build up these walls
The little shards that cover my face
Each one strategically placed
So you can't see what it's hiding
Or how hard I'm truly fighting
For behind that wall my face would show
The pain and memories I undergo
Yet no one really wants to see
The scars that truly made me, me
And so I'll stay behind the mask
The little shards of my glass
That broke apart from me long ago
And no longer got the chance to grow

11. Can You Break Fate?

Can you break fate?
When life makes you want to wait
Yet finding him is what your heart longs for
And no longer wishes to be ignored

Can you make your choice?
When all the noises drown out your voice
And all you hear are those around
Yet even then you feel confound

Can you face your heart?
When you've tried to get it to start
But all it took was his gaze
That made you finally break that daze

Can you choose desire?
As those flames reach higher
And the burns set deep in your soul
Can you take control?

Or will you let the world dictate
Each decision that you make
Until none are left on your plate
And the wheel of your life is no longer fate

Or choose the option your heart is fighting
And let your passion keep igniting
The flame he lit deep inside
And let fate continue to guide

12. I Love Hard and Deep

I love hard and deep
Much like a sloth loves to sleep
Yet with all the love I give there's still
A missing piece left to fill
And I began to fear my puzzle forever incomplete
For who can love someone new to her feet?
As I learn to navigate this new life of mine
Who could love a girl so confined?
For my past is hard to escape
No man can save me, not even with a cape.
Yet I can't expect a savior
Not with all my past failures
And who I used to be
Although not many have ever seen
The girl that hid behind that door
Scared of living anymore
Yet dreams of a home she wants to see
Where she's able to be her true "me"
With no shame to bring her down
And she's able to wear her crown
Yet who would care to see her past
With all that broken glass
That covers her all around
With no path to be found.

So yes I may love hard and deep
But does it matter if no one wants to keep
My heart the way it lays right now
No one should have to take that vow
For my darkness can be too much to take
And no one should have to live with my mistakes.

13. The Calm Before the Storm

You are the calm before the storm
And the beauty that rises after.
You are the ocean waves as they form
And the sand they crash and scatter.
You are the way life feels
And the way it shouldn't matter
Yet even when we reveal
Our life is broken and shattered
You remind us You are even the storm
And there is not one You have not mastered.

14. Beauty

"Beauty is in the eye of the beholder"
Yet what about that of the molder?
Can beauty only be dignified skin deep,
Much like wool only regarded on sheep?
No one refers to beauty of the heart,
Or how beautiful it is to be smart.
No, the skin is referred to as beautiful,
While the others remain disputable.
However, it seems, surface beauty is easy to fake
As outside appearances are easy to make
Yet inner beauty speaks truth
Of someone's heart and youth
And the work they put into their soul
To help them continue to remain whole.
Yet how funny is it that,
The more someones soul seems to lack
Their appearance takes a plunder
Doesn't it make you wonder?
Or when a person shines from within
You can see that glow on their skin
And that beauty radiates their appearance
Without any interference
Remember outer beauty fades away
When we wake up old and grey

With our heart only left to show
Just how beautiful we did grow.

15. This Life

I can not express the life that we hold
Not always filled with emeralds rubies or gold
But in memories and moments that hold more meaning
Than trinkets and things that can be demeaning
This life that we live, though very hard,
Can still toss out some good cards
For the sun chose to shine on you today
Even if yours may be stuck behind some grey
So remember the worth this life holds
Even here without any gold
Your life holds meaning, even if you can't see
Your life is why some people still be
So find your reasons, there are plenty there
To be your why and help when you're in despair
Because your life's meaning is beautiful and bold
And once again, you have no idea how much it truly holds.

16. A Smile a Day

A smile a day can chase the pain away
Yet when I'm here my heart smiles with no fear
For laughter pushes a smile to surface
And in these moments my laugh has purpose
For I feel seen in ways I have never
Even in moments I attempt to be clever
When wit is met with equaled laughter
It does not matter what happens after
For the smile I gaze can fill me for days
And the warmth I feel has helped me heal
So it is in this place I have been
With the company of that handsome grin
Where the earth begins to wait
While we take time to create
Though the future makes no promises
And can seem a little ominous
I see no dark clouds in your eyes
And I have no intention of any goodbyes
Only to keep you close to me
Where I feel I can finally breathe.

17. Not my Normal

I lie, wilted and alone, not knowing where to stand.
Days I've had no one, but then you grabbed my hand.
And I reached to pull away thinking I should be alone,
Until you grabbed my other, and reminded me how Ive grown.
Yet, I still feel wilted in ways that need to heal.
Especially on days you truly make me feel.
For I am not used to the way your presence engulfs me,
Or the way it feels when your arms set me free.
For violence has been a constant in my life,
Pressed against me, the blade to a knife.
Yet after a while, the pressure brings its own form of solace.
A comfort in that unbroken promise.
Where nightmares feel like dreams,
Ones where I no longer scream.
But that knife is now removed,
And left, an unsightly bruise.
Relief from any future threats,
And yet it's still hard to forget.
In times where the knife would dig deeper,
I can feel myself growing weaker.
And reverting to fear and silence like before,
Preparing for that anger that would normally pour.

But with you the anger never comes,
Even as my body numbs.
Yet your comfort feels like needles at times,
As your kisses brush my bruised lines.
The sting of the uncertainty
Causing my body's urgency
And as each kind word spoken should bring peace,
Instead a new fear is being released.
For what if this is the act,
And there will be a day where it will crack?
A new blade against my scar,
Somehow that seems less bizarre,
Then the thought of this kindness being what's normal,
Being so new, it must just be formal.
So I wait for the thick fog to steal my air,
In moments where I am left unaware,
Like an old friend whose presence is unwelcome,
But now is no longer seldom.
However as that fog continues to lack,
And does not currently attack,
I want to believe this is how it will always be,
Even if it's not the normal I have seen.

18. Fear's Happiness

Why does fear control in moments happiness should
prevail?
Why must I feel alone to no avail?
I dream of happiness being brought to me
Yet once here, I am anything but free
For the worlds cruel thoughts encumber my brain
And place me under so much strain
And yet the bustle continues through
With little left of me to brew
And the worlds sweet somber
As I'm left to ponder
What my life has left to give
If even in happiness I can not live
For I am used to the corruption that comes after
And how that leads toward disaster
Or the revelation that the happiness was a front
Until the knife cut regardless of being blunt
So now I choose to see
How happiness was portrayed to be
There until the glass breaks
And then there's nothing left for me to take.

19. Find Herself

She's trying to find herself in a half beaten track
Not sure exactly what it is that she lacks
she's never felt the touch of loving hands
No matter what shes done, she never stands a chance.

She sends a prayer to the good Lord above
Hoping and praying for a good man to love
Who can show her how her life can be
To be with someone who can set love free.

She's a good girl, she knows how to be used
She won't fight it because she's already bruised
And when the world keeps pushing she already knows

It's Her love that may be hard to expose
But she'll get up and stand everyday
Praying this bad luck would just go away
No matter what it is Yall to choose to see
The only thing she wants is to be free

20. Prayers Prayed

Prayers prayed have their way of shaming me
Yet I still pray for one day I hope to see
The life I wished to hold so close
The one I pray that means the most
For riches can fix outer troubles
Yet it is inner ones that make me stumble
The rush and surges that heed no warnings
Much like blisters when they start forming
But hope does not lack in my heart
Nor has it lacked from the start
And I still pray one day I'll see it form
That dream I've longed to transform
For now in my head the story plays
Like a melody that forever stays
So I'll hum a verse now and then
To feel that dream once again
Till daytime breaks and the night is gone
Yet it is that song that I will still long

21. Our Story in the Stars

So dark is the night sky,
Yet meadows I still see in your eyes.
Blinded by the stars so bright
Their fire our only light
Yet the one that burns within me
Helps me see you so clearly
And to hear your words spoken in my head
The constellations of the things you said
And the ringing of your laughter
Or even the sounds you make after
Push my heart to skip again
And sometimes even count to ten
But the way the stars tell their stories,
Through tragedy and worries,
Leaving an impending doom
One that continues to loom
Yet the love they told,
even if old,
Still prove a forever
Regardless of failed endeavors
So forgive me as I stare at the stars
Wondering which ones might be ours
And praying that it's story holds no tragedy
Yet only one of vitality

And as that constellation continues to build
I hope it's our hearts that's fulfilled
For stories only tell a small variety
But with you I want its entirety.